RIBBONS OF LIGHT

POENZA

DP Porreca

New Beagle
PUBLISHING

RIBBONS OF LIGHT
POENZA
DP Porreca

Published by New Beagle Publishing
A Division of Beagle Holdings, LLC.
9820 Willow Creek Road, Suite 220
San Diego, CA 92131
858.547.9682
858.547.9685 (fax)

10 9 8 7 6 5 4 3 2 1

ISBN 0-9759993-0-3

Printed in the United States of America
Cover Photo: Gary Irving
Design: The DavidHenry Agency

RIBBONS OF LIGHT | POENZA

ACKNOWLEDGEMENTS

Two wonderful books---"Native American Wisdom", edited by Kent Nerburn and Louise Mengelkoch, and "The Myths of the North American Indians", by the legendary Lewis Spence, were principal references that inspired the indigenous-themed poetry in this book.

As with "Sixty2", the leading cosmologists, physicists, logicians, cognitive and neuro-scientists---who together form the nucleus of our generation's best and brightest---- continue to inspire me with their research, discoveries, insights, and as always---their matter-of-fact humility.

A special thanks to The DavidHenry Agency, which accomplishes all the design-through-production work, and of course to Dona, my wonderful wife, editor, and champion in life.

TABLE OF CONTENTS

I. GATEWAYS

A NEW PACIFIC CENTURY

I.

As the sun sets, golden red,
the Pacific's shimmer promises
a resplendent dawn.

The quiet, as a mirror, reflects
on ageless hopes and fears,
opportunities squandered.

What is it about our dreams,
which seem inevitably to
lead to nightmares?

Nightmares of history,
perturbed and distorted ideas,
draperied as progress.

Nightmares of activism,
realized as repressions of
freedom and liberty.

Nightmares of movements,
prisons of the mind, robed
as equality and justice.

Nightmares of conformity,
in the re-education camps
and academic committees.

II.

The theocrats argue and die
over the correct way to
worship God.

The social engineers fight
to make everyone equally
subservient and sterile.

The pundits discuss the
minutiae of dialog, evading
the essence of substance.

Technology advances, aiding
and alienating, as wisdom
and reflection decline.

Science reveals wondrous
unseen worlds and fabrics
of a new reality---

even as it participates
in the reckless proliferation
of hideous weaponry.

In a laboratory, stem
cell research promises
exponential advance

in the fight against
debilitating diseases and
the accidents of inheritance.

But, this too is stymied by
religious belief systems
uninformed by reason,

partisan politics encouraged
by a duplicitous media,
and the circus of ignorance.

III.

On a mountain summit,
living alone, in the
silence of meditation,

an eastern monk sees
the sun rise over these
same Pacific waters.

4

His only visitor, the
sound of light rain settling
in the bamboo thicket.

His dreams are of
contingency and chance,
the inseparable nature

of all that is in life,
of life and of the cosmos---
undivided by artificiality.

Artificiality of boundaries,
mere categorical perceptions
of our limited senses.

Artificiality of perfection,
the curious need in humans
to ascribe to states of divinity,

which would be sterile, rather
than transcendent, void
rather fulfilling.

Artificiality of knowledge,
the confusion between beliefs,
proofs, and experience.

IV.

And as the rain lifts,
to greet the shining
new day of radiance,

he too reflects on who
we are, what we have become,
and what we yet may be.

But unlike his counterpart,
of the other construct, he
sees the wholeness,

more than the parts---
the bewildering array of
consciousness's fragments.

He experiences the web
of life and connectedness
to the cosmos' eternity,

the cycle of change,
the sanctity of mystery,
and the peace of reflection.

He will not advance the
state of scientific art, nor
master technology's processes;

but what he may just do, is
uncover the essential meaning---
which eludes us all.

BROKEN TRAIL

I

High above the coast,
dubbed "California Riviera",
the modernity and the mansions,
another world resides.

Ranches and ranchitas, but
mainly trailer homes and cabins,
the artifacts of history,
still linger in the dust.

The record is alive,
in the lifestyle and the people,
experiencing the daily struggle,
as reflections of our myths.

Is self-reliance dead,
or a product of fiction's excess,
an historical illusion,
to ease a nation's angst?

To inform your own opinion,
you may want to take a
journey, high into a past,
stubbornly kept alive today.

Don't rely on experts,
the pundits and researchers,
in academic settings,
untouched by nature's ways.

Experience takes some effort,
but the reward is worth the sweat,
besides, you already know, the
political flavor of your daily feed.

II

Instead, jump into a four-wheel,
seek out Refugio Road, drive
high into the mountains,
and above our culture below.

There you may meet history,
or a little derivative slice,
being lived by real people,
dedicated to some intrinsic---

which elites describe as fiction,
or antiquity in understanding,
though others still appreciate it,
for its economy and its soul.

It is both spare and simple,
but the people are not either,
many educated, but dissatisfied
with choices deemed mundane.

For them, some words have
meaning, are not merely slogans,
and cynicism in their life, has
neither value nor refrain---

like liberty and justice, or
just helping out a friend,
or rights and obligations
to each other and the land.

Take a ride on horseback,
or hire out for just a day,
you may discover something
that will surprise you still.

I know you've heard the lectures,
in the halls of academe,
the revised interpretations and
the bilge of post-modern swill,

but don't you think it wise,
to experiment as well,
have a frame of reference, not
cloaked in correctness garb?

If you are open to the moment,
and willing to examine beliefs,
the stereotypes may be vanquished,
that you better understand yourself.

III

For there is an American experience,
distinct from an imperialist role,
and it's not the brazen shallowness,
or immorality, as you were told.

It's always most surprising,
and exciting to the mind,
to find a better people still
exist in narcissistic times.

The memetic groan of media,
the sameness of their smile,
their ignorance of nature and all
sciences worth the name,

cannot reprise the wisdom,
of those free of mind,
the re-education camps
not fully yet primetime.

Gather your own evidence,
it is the scientific way,
just another reason, for
the correctness cops to bay.

From coast to shining coast,
you will find pragmatists exist,
the ranting of elitists,
having marginal success.
The immigrants still come,

risking all in great pursuit,
of freedoms holy grail,
and the right to its reward.

It was equal opportunity,
not equality of political dole,
that led them to this place,
and marked them for their role.

IV

It's still the greatest experiment,
in government and protected rights,
this mottled complex land,
with its diversity and free speech.

Whatever faults it has, and it has
large ones to be fair, it is not
for want of spirit, or the groundwork
our founders laid so bare.

If there is a threat to liberty,
it will come from within,
an illiberal university more dangerous,
than all the other deadly sins.

So, leave your misconceptions
back at the ivy door, learn
to meet some people you've been
shielded from before.

The left coast and the right coast,
control the networks rabble,
but the internet has freed us all,
from the filters of their babble.

It's really kind of messy,
some opinion is insane,
but it frees from the tyranny
of academia's inane.

Reach out into the country,
meet someone unlike you,

before the campus is unionized
and education through.

The unreconstructed left,
and fundamentalist right,
both dangers to us all,
their absolutes a blight.

But the far left's more the threat,
to the individualist dream,
for free thinking is the target,
of their latest ugly scheme.

If you think this is too harsh,
ask them to kindly explain,
how Vietnam's re-education camps,
are not concentration camps---

and who hid that ugly shame?

AN OLD HINDU TALE

I.

Something that changes everything,
that indefinable quality, an essence
of knowing. What was it?

Was there something ephemeral,
a communication, a metamorphic
signal of decipher?

The ancient mystic said of the cosmos
that no one knows how to unveil,
the deep mystery of creation.

Can there be some singular entity,
God as being, as existence and essence,
metamorphic in transcending existence?

If there existed some entity,
some immaterial spirituality,
from where would come the material,

the material of the material world,
which through organic chemistry
and the shock of the lightening strike,

brought forth the incubus of life:
the broth of replication that gave us
all in our nature, our beginning?

Eternity must mean eternity. The material
of matter and consciousness arose over the eons
of transformation, change, and adaptation.

If it is posited that spontaneous raw material
grew from the atomization of a singularity,
the hypothesis of extant-God is unnecessary.

If a cause needs an intelligent prime mover
of spiritual existence, than an infinite regress
into non-existence is reason's logical trap.

The poetry of the mystic was of beauty,
a mysterious harmonic of understanding,
cosmos and nature as undivided consequences

of the same hidden processes,
endlessly repeated over the eons of time
and the reincarnations of the fundamental force.

II.

Yes, the science was imprecise and limited,
but the metaphors easily march to the
logic, as the multiverse of universes,

the same atoms of the singularity, being
re-distributed in form and function
by the wondrous chaos of chemistry and physics.

More than thousands of years ago, long
before the near-east's tribes hear
voices presumed divine, in a more

ancient and meditative culture, of
circles and hidden dimensions, rather
than hierarchies and behavioral laws,

a culture's best minds, mathematically
and cosmically inclined, found a window
into understanding that eludes most today.

What spark of insight did they receive?
Was it something of their culture's form,
or a dance of atoms playing notes of meaning?

What causes lesser of them now to lose
their way? The detritus of religious
wars now rampaging in their breast.

III.

Around the globe a return to bitter
fruit hastens its ugly stampede, a
new force of the indoctrinated to the fore.

In wailing calls for prayer, amidst the beauty
of stained glass artistry and melodies, in centers of
harsh penitence and morbid fear,

those that followed a different path continue
to flail in the error of that shattered
path, and reap the discriminations of ignorance.

Though many express a cultural affinity for
practices and observances their cult profess,
the scaffold's existence imbues the most extreme,

to die for practiced difference, immaterial
to a legitimacy or reasoned cause, simply
as means to idea's control and freedom's end.

Others cling to some solemn word, that
God has chosen only them, to possess
this land, and rule over it for him.

The papists and their offspring call for
peace, but deny science tools to cure
humanity and redress social injustice.

Someone states, "look at all
the good that's done", but all merely footnote,
to the ethics and the morals of the Greeks.

IV.

The music and cathedrals, the temples,
and the mosques, all promise children
of the earth a life that glorifies death.

When will the new chimpanzees take
the final step and free themselves

from the bondage of their past?

Was it evolution's choice, that this
module in our head, would pre-dispose
us to superstition's ugly cloth?

I do not know how far our journey can
hoist the weight of this grievous error,
and this horrendous crippling trait.

But of one thing I am sure, if I believed
in prayer---- it would be to recreate,
this now told old Hindu tale anew.

SUNSET IN SANTA BARBARA

Your lies will rust your soul,
seek out your weakest trait,
to manufacture defining tests.

You will insist it's merely luck,
the providence of chance, not
predestined star-crossed events.

But you will be unsure,
knowing nature's ways are veiled,
in landscapes of infinite folds----

perhaps, suspending time's constraints,
searching and reveling in the possibilities
and permutations of myriad states?

Free will consists of choices,
not unlimited or unconstrained,
but in the alternatives of the moment;

in the landscapes of the present,
the delimited consciousness of now,
----not imagined meadows of virginal foam.

The playing fields of scale, narrowing
predictive outcome and welcoming
possibility's role in quantum recesses,

might well apply in life's context,
the immensity of smallness, weirder than
the immensity of infinity itself.

So, who is to mark our scale, dear
reader and friend, in this universe of
bewildering strings and harmonies,

a multiverse of dimensions and laws,
so manifestly beautiful, yet
logically humbling and chaotic?

What do you think, when alone----
about the choices never considered,
or the bad ones repeatedly exercised?

Why does the unfair hand,
seem so disproportionately dealt,
but so regularly recurrent,

for some, rather than for others,
over the course lines of event-filled
lives, of melodramatic content?

Is it predestined or predisposed, some
non-local entanglement of expression,
with the strange attractors in the landscape?

Or is the algorithm of consciousness,
as blind as the algorithm of evolution,
and merely an image of our own illusion?

Breathe in the sunset, await the darkness,
the illumination of the cosmos,
its billions of stars sharing their secrets,

reach out to touch them with your mind
and your soul together--- and then let
their music astound you with their answer.

THE BEACH AT BACARA

A wild windswept beach,
the central California coast,
driftwood bleached and poignant.

Two lives reflect on pasts,
divergences and choice,
the bitter and unanswerable.

How did it come to this,
a life of love and joy,
extent from all so wretched?

In truth we never know,
how fortune lights the path,
for seekers of the Sun.

Some to crash amidst
the surf of storm tossed
seas, in unrequited sorrow,

while others grasp the
fruit, of passion's enduring
quest, an undivided soul.

THE QUARTER HORSE

From horseback, the world looks different,
remembrances of heroic struggles,
flood the imagination.

The westward trek, seeks discovery's face,
not the prologue of mere greed,
but a primal dream.

It is now known, the genetic trace clear,
we are descendants of a migratory species,
innately transient.

Our civilizations, since pre-history's time,
desire the far horizon, the transforming act,
not mere economic quest.

From mountain trails, in Pacific's view,
interpretations are challenged, emotions
charged with need.

The need is visceral, opportunities call,
as much excuse as rational choice, this
pull of the west.

A manifest destiny, of evolutionary instinct,
a preface to knowing the meaning of us, and
a realization of self.

PLATITUDES

He stumbled down the slope
of the jagged narrow ravine
into the quiet of the desert night.

The coyotes' distant howl
a reminder of the descent,
and how weak he had become.

His throat was dry and parched,
his body hurt and spent,
through dark enfolding pain.

One errant moment's chance
turned to tragic waste,
two friends-- near death in dust.

The guard rail was too weak
the van careened and leapt,
the silence shattered in the sound.

One too many drinks, the old
lodge's last round beckoned,
joy to terror at shadow's edge.

He now searches for a light,
some vacant hope he'll find,
the saving help in time.

Of all the thoughts that race,
through dim requited space,
the last heard words remind

of all its fated ugly game.
Bob, the barkeep's close, the
heartfelt platitude, except for
those of cynical dispose.

"Now make sure you guys choose
the right designated driver."

JACK RABBIT

Under a creosote bush,
the shadow partially masks
the outline of its presence.

As the temperature soars,
the midday heat shimmers
in the folds of altered states.

The patterns of chance inflect,
as the click startles the prey
and hesitation seals its fate.

The hunter is rewarded, in his
lens the profile, all perfectly
captured, with an aim that's true.

The timeless perfect kill, a digital
image, the bloodless moment of
state, the trophy immortally taken.

VIEW FROM FONT'S POINT

The purple spills to rust,
the washes splayed as
myriad fingers stretching
out toward the salted sea.

As sunset fades to reddened
swirls of tufted vapor, the
coyotes cross the paths where
moccasin tracks are unseen.

No one sees the animal spirits
that parade in celebration below,
except those who are someone in
union with a place of sentient soul.

Who was the last to see them,
whose being depends on the
imagination of nature's wholeness,
not the particulars of its fragments?

Rub the piece of wood, listen
to its music and hear its message,
not of syllables and words, but
of sacred feelings and remembrances.

As night descends and the dark enfolds,
listen still for that magic breath,
first heard as the infant's entrance,
into the blinding white light of becoming.

Is it not still there, in the wood
and in the stone, preserved forever,
as not the nothing of some thing, but
the dreamtime of someone, as you?

FEBRUARY RAINS

I.

The rains began early this year,
bringing with them the promise
of wild flowers in profusion by April.

The desert sky by winter knew
what nature's intent bespoke,
as curtains of grey awoke the silence.

To clearly see the desert bloom,
imagination must flee the edge
of sentient grasp and reflexive bound.

The categories of distinction, as
in Chopin's first concerto, yield to
the dance of creatures yet discovered..

What did he see as paradise lost
in flashing moments before death?
Is the Sabbath of muted luminosity

dead, in pyres of modernity's debris,
washed as souls in costumed dress,
in arroyos latent with suspended life?

Does the idea of the idea, precede
the oboe's solo in Mozart's moment
as the theme unwinds its evolve, or

is the archetype present in the
folded union of the conceived whole,
entangled lifeless awaiting birth?

II.

The ghosts of possibility, as dwarfs
in human constellations reveal, a
difference yet sameness in asymmetry.

The oneness of scale in detail's robe
descends to variation in representation's
disrobe, as expectation masks the missing.

Are men merely made of their words,
as their own, or as spoken of them,
as cuisine is made of ingredients apart;

categorized cuisine, as much
thematically as in representational sense,
to be other than common recipe?

Space is not Euclidean, and simultaneity
not absolute, yet the clockwork determinism
enfolds the mind's eye sense of things.

Truth and relativism co-existent in logic
at different scales, but the arguments
concerning objectivity and subjectivity

rage, as if the invariance is scale independent
and the Aristotelian categories of understanding
remain inviolate and immune to statistical law.

Are belief and desire simply "folk psychology",
or are intuitions too entangled as systems to
reveal their separable parts in crisp categories?

Necessity and contingency, the gradations
of awareness all blend in disarray of
sets and bounds not neatly classical.

The concrete structures of our senses
may be instead those of our imagination,
hidden by dimensions unobserved but real.

III.

As the rains of February turn to torrents
in the wilderness of the Anza-Borrego,
the possibility of radiant fields of

golden and purple flowers is enhanced.
If you wander near in April, off the trail
well-traveled, your journey may be worthy.

Often in the crevices, along old arroyo banks,
the carpets of the flowers flow like
discarded robes of fallen angels,

covering the barren earth, and reflecting
sunlight shadows in the twilight's
lingering, as reflected burnished haze.

If you see a moment of this glory's light,
flash before you in the instant, will you be
open to its presence and its meaning?

And if you don't experience this moment,
being denied its eternal beauty, will you search
again next year, or merely insist it does not exist?

WINDOWPANES

Can we trust the senses,
rain as points of choice,
droplets pool as waves?

The grey dawn roils,
into black foam,
a system's prediction.

Causal effects, faster
than light's speed, not
relativity's universe.

Identify the instant,
the gateway opens,

a configuration, but
not intrinsic time?

The equations swirl,
the thunderheads unfurl,
the cymbals are entangled.

Direction, not dimension,
each point distinctly fated,
kissing logic's choice.

Decision states, and triangles,
fractals in the mists,
static waves in colors.

Can we ever know,
the mystery of equations,

abstracted from the realm,
spinning in wetware, and

drowning in the storm,
of yet another capsule?

II. DIMENSIONS IN TIME

ANOTHER TIME

{for Ohiyesa}

I.

On a remote mountain,
in the stillness of snow,

an ancient tribe described
the ways of its Mothers:

"The imminent birth
of a child, is the advent

of a hero, to the poetic
mind, a spiritual event."

She comes alone to
this in silence, her

meditations are to
instill spiritual influence,

from the moment of birth.
"It's love, it's love,

the fulfilling life,
bringing to the receptive

soul, the love of the
Great Mystery, and the

sense of connectedness
with all of creation!"

II.

In a sullen city,
in another time,

the emergency room
attendant screams

loudly and intolerantly,
that a very pregnant

woman's paper work,
is incorrect and incomplete,

amidst the cacophony
of civilization's howl,

and the indifference
of a jaded age.

III.

In the land of Ghosts,
Ohiyesa's tears

flow like the rivers,
down through the

clouds in torrents
of pure despair.

All that he knew
of the white man's

ways, his lack of
holiness and of spirit,

have painfully become
the path of many.

How will the land, the
essence of humanity,

its womb robed
in the Great Mystery,

and ultimately---
the soul itself endure?

BEGINNINGS

The child of time, new day evolves,
the river of ideas, flooding the senses.

The magic of colors, a wondrous world,
the scent of flowers, imprints the life.

But what of the darkness, an impoverished
place, without warming sun,
the magic dissolved?

The winter of soul, harsh in example,
the fate of one's life,
the province of chance.

How does one rise, above the experience,
the dawn of trace, knowing despair?

The imprint remains, unlearn the lessons,
the wiring adaptive, to experience's change.

An indistinct moment, forms the new fractal,
yesterday's shadows, deep in retreat.

Prepare the earth, the dance is beginning,
the circus of life, newly renewed.

Listen to songlines, refrain from the ashes,
ontology's transform,
and precursor to strength.

CANADIAN TUNDRA

Silent forests, glaciered hills,
illusive signposts, shrouded
in mist.

The frontier, without bounds,
of the mind, innate to
human awareness.

Ancient paths, migrations' scent,
hunting trails, of spirit
and need.

The need to know, to seek
the sun, the verdant meadow,
and last horizon.

Destiny speaks, eons tell,
of human quests to
understand.

The need transcends, the genetic
mandate, emergent from
adaptive choice.

A higher plane, of desire
and want, a luminous valley
of consciousness.

The ribbons of light, the
settled sun, the beginning
of knowing

who and what we are,
descends like shadows
on the moon,

and stirs the emotion,
sounding the primal chord
of discovery.

CHIEF BLUE COYOTE

He who paints of faces,
vermilion split by blue,
rhythmic and intricate still.

Irregular, but patterned,
as the spirit in all things,
which is the weave of life.

The chief's divided face,
in symbolism's colors told
of anguish yet unseen.

From the mud of nothing
they arose, a culture honoring
the great spirit and mystery.

But from out of the east
would come, in numbers
too vast to properly convey,

a tribe of white-faced men,
with knowledge magical
to learn and behold.

But also, without sense of
spirit or soul-- meaning
absent from its knowing.

And thus he said, "Our world
would end, the buffalo
laid dead in snow,

the prairies stretched no
more, and eagle's
nest in saddened

wind, emptied of its
breath, as drifts in
black mourning shroud,

the last flutes' notes upon
the setting sun of freedom,
whispering the warriors end".

The time before nothing
returns, and the red man's
day becomes nothing again.

They had their time, and
they did well by following
nature's wisdom and sound.

The new clan will bring
much, but also destroy
so very much in its path.

Only time will tell if
this new tribe can
see and hear as well as act.

If the sacred is gone,
can what remains have
purpose or bring any joy?

"Look to the face-painters
in the future" said the Chief.
"Their signs will answer you".

COYOTE GULCH

Drums in echo, ancient spirits,
waterless arroyos,
the scent of sagebrush.

The sad-eyed Chief,
alone in colors,
vestiges of another time.

A modern world, awash
in chaos, splintered values
from serpent tongues.

The wind and fire,
a muted palace,
the cliff's vermilion

hued by the sun,
above enchanted
once sacred valleys.

When did the spirit,
leave the land,
and turn the river dry,

creation's river bled of
life, haunted towers
in red repose?

The noble dream,
buried in sand,
the shaman's chant silent.

The coyote's howl,
anguished lament, in
lost states of grace,

and promises gone,
amidst eternal waves
of old ochre sands.

NATIVE WISDOM

This endless cycle of change,
this life of things--

the physicist seeks to explain
the entanglement of particles,

random collisions which impart
characteristics once separable,

now linked in weird unity,
forever holistically joined,

though discrete in space-time,
unified by their attributes.

This new quantum understanding
disrupts relativity's foundation,

the future and present as one:
time not merely background,

processes unfolding as computations,
perhaps-- the real atoms of

the universe, and a feature of
all living and inanimate things.

Chief Blue Coyote once said,
"The Great Mystery is one,

and all things are one--
the Great Spirit, the earth

and the land, and all of
nature's living things,

a harmony of the connected whole,
their identities separated only by

shapes and forms and the
colors of painted faces---

for our amusement and the
peace of mind it brings us."

MYTHS AND CONSTRAINTS

The lonely haunting flute,
the indigenous sounds and ways,
stories clothed in sadness.

Do all tribes know of the fruit,
the forbidden golden pear,
the apple and serpent?

Far away from the rising sun,
Feather-woman loves the
Morning Sun,

and is teleported to
the domain of Gods, and her
eternal fate.

For though in paradise,
with someone held so dear,
temptation does prevail.

The Great Turnip is uprooted,
as we all must with curiosity know,
what is denied by fear.

What impulse so prevails,
that knowledge's thirst is ever
prime and unrequited?

What fear in culture seeks,
to ever punish those who defy
the shaman's edict?

The seeker of the tale is
inevitably punished with remorse,
and paradise is lost.

But dear reader, I do ask
what paradise is this that
punishes our curiosity so?

Is it not sad that ideas
are not thought as rivers--
bounded yes, but free to flow,

and that shamans cannot
suppress their need for control,
as puppeteers in tow?

For in the end it seems,
that all we hold most dear
has come to us through those

who have shown the courage,
not the fear, to seek the
very truth that leads us

to the paths of inquiry:
to know, be unafraid of seeing,
and to be sanctified by truth.

REGIONS OF THE HEAVENS

The indigenous ones, on the plains
heard the Thunder Gods' roar,

two destinations after death,
different, but absent of dread.

One of Ghosts, neither invulnerable
nor immortal, but heroes of

another time, still hunting, fishing,
and enjoying former delights.

The other of the Super-beings,
the powers of the spirit world,

and all the forces known to
be of nature's Great Mystery.

There was no place of punishment,
for the deities were forgiving.

Souls of scoundrels were welcome
there, for a desert it would be,

the deities themselves they
knew, are also sometimes perverse.

The missionaries called them savages,
for such a malevolent view,

perfection was the order
of the world, so the Padres said.

The indigenous ones, had a difficult
time understanding how this could be,

for witnesses of nature could clearly
see, how mischievous were the Spirits.

Blue Coyote never trusted the Padres,
for he believed them mostly blind,

to humanity's and nature's ways,
and how the two entwined.

"The White Man even argues over
God", he said, "How can that be?"

I wonder what he would have said,
had he been told of the Inquisition,

or lived to see our modern "beliefs",
spiritual intolerance, and the mothers

celebrating the suicidal missions of
their precious children---

all undertaken for the "glory of God"?

THE SECRETS OF GHOSTS

The past and future, as particles entangled,
speak to us through hidden signs,

revealed too briefly, in the wave function's
collapse, invisible to the intentioned senses.

Small fragments of truth, suspend as fractal
memes, morphing through dimensions of time,

piercing the fragment of the beating membrane,
humming the computational music of the cosmos.

As background radiation, imprints of the history
exist indefinitely, in both the past and future,

but the web of connective consciousness, with
synapses distended, widens our chasm of experience.

How did ancient ways, ear to ground, eye to
sky, unveil the texture of the fabric---

that same robe of reality, so presently opaque,
to the structure of its pearl's sheen and tone?

The dust of life, scale and gravity's drooping
eyelids, screen us from the hues, forms melting

and drowning appearance, understanding
clouded by horizons of the imagination.

Did knowledge die in the swamps of religious
dogma, or the miasma of tired metaphors?

Did the functionalism of parts obscure
the dance and fluidity of the whole?

Or did the intruder's massacre of the spirit's
souls, forever bury the mind's secrets?

SNAKE RIVER

Above the raging torrents,
the thunderstorm's retreat,
the canyon's breath in mourning.

The tribesmen showed the way,
shared their precious resource,
and led their spirit to doom.

Their instinct was too generous,
their courtesy misunderstood,
their yield seen as weakness.

Not by the expedition,
but those who would follow,
seeking plunder not discovery.

Across a fabled sea,
in an ancient land,
shattered tribes doubt intent.

This epoch's sincerity is
lost and trampled, by
rhetoric and belief,

the stoic presence of
bitter lies and brutal
myths of gloried pasts.

Thirty years of tortured
limbs and stillbirth minds
shackled by the dark,

now asked to open
to the skies of freedom's
promise without shape,

the form of security's bonds,
the history of laws,
the trust in ordinary rights.

When will we learn, that which
we have, cannot be bequeathed,
it must be lived and evolved?

THE TOTEM

When he reached puberty,
his father sent him to fast,
and discover his spirit.

He climbed to the mountain's
eastern summit, laid his robe
under a ledge and slept.

He did not eat nor move about
for three days, and would sip
from his water just twice daily.

As the sun arose on the fourth
morning, a blue presence fell
and engulfed him with radiance.

It was neither sandstorm nor cloud,
and just as it lifted, an albescent
shaded coyote stood directly in view.

He asked the coyote if he was
to be his guiding spirit, and the
coyote merely seemed to smile.

When he again asked the coyote,
to show him a sign so he may
know of his understanding's truth,

the spectre vanished from his
sight, and a cold wind enveloped
the ledge, howling in despair.

From that day on, the little
boy needed no words to
interpret the spirit ways,

and as he descended the
mountain with a speed and an
awareness not formerly felt,

he knew from thence he
would be blessed to be---
and be called, "Blue Coyote".

WINTER IN DAKOTA TERRITORY

Across an endless plain-----
a lonesome buffalo,

in sadness searches for
the path,

the thunder of an ancient past,
an echo of the herded scent.

The hooded moon,
preserves the memory,

a wretched deed and
mindless act, or

willful slaughter of
full intent?

For there are many ways
to kill a man----

some more cruel than
by the knife or gun.

The tribes were felled
by disease and greed,

but their totem died
in blood soaked snows,

the wanton act of
ruthless empire,

a crucifixion of
the indigenous soul.

As light snow falls,
in bitter cold,

an old man reads
in lunar lines,

the pockmarked craters
and crevices of tears,

of all that was, and
then was lost,

of which was human
and held so dear.

To know the spirit
of these beasts,

was to know
the true path

of the Great Mystery's
way,

to re-unite in
nature's womb,

and know the heart
of history's doom.

Now only sentinels,
robed as ghosts,

remain to serve
as sainted hosts,

to with the moon
tell the tale,

of humanity's sin
and creation's wail.

For we shall never
see again

a culture of
the fire and wind,

attuned to know of
nature's play,

and as practiced in
its sacred way.

WORMHOLE

I.

A snow-covered peak, the tiny village,
a mountain home, the waves of golden grain.

From granite hills, the peasant fled,
to a larger world, and opportunity's gate.

An empire of blood, the epoch's footprints,
slender roman pines, the warrior's guide.

What did he know, at century's turn,
the modern world, from plow to steam?

The sweat of brow, knows no relief,
the human toil, transcends the task.

In later years, the world condensed,
the global commerce, the smoothing function,

a continent of wars, now joined in union,
animosity's trash, buried by the age.

His sons of sons, now span the globe,
and climb the heights of prominence,

education's promise, and intellectual sweat,
the genes and values, wired intact.

What temporal mind, what common thread,
laid synchronous claim, to concert?

Generations come and gone, but still
the same path traversed.

The trails they walked, obscured by time
and scale of history fleeting,

the noise and rush of empires lost,
and the stench of tyrannies dying.

The empires now, forgotten realms,
a chronology of glory and fame.

Civilization's womb, the birthing place,
of wondrous things and brutal shame.

The civil wars, to empire's reach,
hereditary rule, to meritocracy's beseech,

all these things, the incubus for modern
life, and institutions of future claim.

Lost in telling of the details,
the profusion of intrigues and vice,

the shadows of history's tabloid rites,
which obscure the light of knowledge.

Yes, raw brutal power and cruelty,
the domain of imperialism,

a militaristic collage of the tribes,
the breadth and depth of empire.

But these mappings from the past,
to our metamorphic present age,

do not explain the fragments of,
ideas born of noble aspire,

nor the symmetry of the mind,
through wormholes to the current time,

as revealed in mirrored relief, the
journey through civilization's soul.

II.

Of many generations, before the
ships great depart to distant gates,

to opportunity's modern shore,
his forbearers experience the same.

His many pasts of blood and genes,
led back to the zero of marked time,

clans of clans, ancient in those
granite hills, west of Ionian trespass.

A great-uncle was first of note,
the chroniclers' favorite prologue,

but it was he, of august name,
and conservative nature, who brought

the stature and leadership needed,
as well as the vision of merit.

A stature born of values, commitment
to strong family and ethic code.

Though popular poet, trivialized the
mandate, his stance bore true,

and poet, with daughter, felt the
rebuke of exile's sting.

Of empire sought, there also
grew examples of wisdom's dawn,

populations embraced, tolerance shown,
fostered integration of cultural tribute.

The ultimate triumph would face
the test of hereditary infirmity,

the unfit menace, of sibling greed,
for power and the throne.

The petty world of power-elite,
the trail of festered deceit,

would all play roles in the undoing,
salvaged only by the crippled gait.

That he should rise, the enfeebled one,
of no majesty shown, except the sum

of nurtured mind and learned skill,
a humble countenance, tempered will.

For he was such, that of his time,
institutions grew of varied kind,

which layered the world, with
wizened acts, fairness in the

artifacts of lost civilities from
aimless force, republican in respect.

To be undone, but once again,
of only him only, not the gain,

by the moral philosopher of
his age, the suckling hypocrite.

And though the worst was yet
to come, the fiddling fire to

succumb, the time of heredity's
crown at end, amidst new presage.

A new order from merit's
store, from farther east did

restore, a new century's drive
for unity, amidst a gathered storm.

A leader came to keep the
flame, burning bright in justice's

name, and much was given to
the world, before the dark descent.

And thus from such evil, much
survived, the rule of law to

energize and move the
world to give appeal,

to grander views of man,
awaiting history's next repair.

The cycle worn apart again,
the crown of thorns,

its aftermath, the cape of
apostolic zeal, in transcendence.

Of heroism, and its new reward,
he touching of the mass accord,

to humbler men, and faith,
which would now all engulf.

III.

So, it is written, still
in current time, blood-draped history,

pretext divine, history's stories,
correctness chipped and tattered.

Of awful deeds without recourse,
to context's privilege of discourse,

that ancient names and
attributes fail to find.

They live in modern infamy,
without a trace of posterity,

the dead white ghosts of
academy's gross decline.

The classic force of history,
the dustbin of inequity,

with Egypt, Greece, and Islam's
shared pantomime.

Julius, Augustus, Ovid,
with Julia, Claudius, Seneca.

Nero, the elect Trajan, a note
in lineage's final due,

from which all comes the
cycle's retinue, new age of

religion's dangerous brew, as
ever vicious as the epoch's end.

For as the DNA entwines, the
mistakes of the trail reminds,

us of the frozen state of
time----dimension's time,

that which we learn so little,
from our previous kind.

That as the march of history,
impedes upon the mystery,

the universe's mask, divided moments,
suspend all undivided rhyme.

The monochrome synchronicity,
an artful act of sagacity,

cannot account for space-
and-mind fused braids.

The bearded twine, alive
as then, in spirits of resign

again, the consciousness
submerged in sacred fields.

The future and the past are
one, a point of scale, immediacy,

the beaten drum, the cosmos
string's vibrating song survives.

Too faint to know, too strong to
soothe, the shadow's afterglow

infused, by all the dreams,
the hopes and bitter tears.

It's to the light, the trail leads,
the path of human frailties,

the supreme role of
courage through the years.

Wisdom is to grace the core,
forever forward to explore,

the baseless narrow
paths of primal fears.

For evolution shows the way,
the cosmos artful robed display,

annealing of the sense's call,
to blindness and dismay.

Time non-existent in divorce,
dimensions hidden from the fall,

all robed in fragments of a force, all
from the spiral's dark array.

Matter masked by luminous
gas, particles swimming in the vast

immensity of the crumpled sphere,
the cosmic form, and form's decay.

For it's only through the warp
of space, the wormhole of

our human race, that
life itself, is seen as life, at all.

TIMELESSNESS

{for Julian Barbour}

Many-colored mists, landscapes of the possible,
stacked as sheaves of wheat, vertical to the plain.

Dynamic to the eye, motion set in pictures,
snapshots of the instance, touched by points of rain.

Plato's fields of types, the endless mirrors of history,
illusions of the senses, the need for capsule form.

The arrow points direction, not dimensions curved
in space, escape from geometrics, relativity's embrace.

The ancients walked the troughs, the ice cave of the mind,
sentient being's awareness, a framework of its kind.

Is it in the music, the music of the primes, or does it
rest in values of computation's steep incline.

The static point of states, in configuration's flux,
the eigenvalues mating in probability's dense redox.

The persistence of the objects, not easily cast aside,
the arguments on motion, the Kantian reside?

Perhaps it is the flavors, of observer and observed,
the consciousness of flavors, the boundaries all obscured?

The subjective little snapshots, interpretations of
all there is, motion as illusion, intrinsic time a whim.

But do we all remember the illusion of the spin,
the curve ball does not curve, it spun from similar kin.

The poles were set apart, Bob Feller took the ball,
and proved to startled physicists it did curve after all.

But if Julian is right, and we can't dismiss the claim,
there are no laws of nature, but of universe to name.

And in our timeless states, the capsule is innate,
it is the role of wind, to point to God's estate.

III. THE DIVIDED MIND

THE TWO HEMISPHERES

I.

The swollen creek obscures
the trail, as the cactus bloom
suspends the logic's edge.

The Ancient Greeks struggled
with the knowing of the good,
the true, and the eternal beauty.

The mind apart of nature's
way descends the path of
twisted shape and focus.

The liberal enlightenment sought
governing principles; of equality,
truth, democracy and justice.

The boasting ram bellows
his song, as ocotillo paint
the mountainside's shadow.

Modernity's dignity left in
ashes, under constant attack
by the constructionist's folly.

The tamarisk grove hides
the dens of nocturnal creatures
awaiting the night's primal close.

The misreading of Kuhn,
paradigm's meaning, leads to
the abyss of discovery's truth.

He ascends the trail
near the oasis breaks,
as coyotes howl in chorus.

Post-modernity emerges
as reaction to science, and the
death of the great chain of being.

The higher he climbs, the
harder the mind is challenged
to know the unnatural way.

Post-modernity believes, theories
exist, for sociological reason,
independent of evidence's need.

The rattlers slither along
a broken path, a hobbled
rabbit, leaving its bloody stain.

Perception and explanation are
on equal plane with empiricism,
all frameworks of equal worth.

An eagle drifts in noiseless vapor,
alert to dramas of chance unfolding
in purple canyons deep below.

Interpretation is divorced from
method, theories' merits
judged by temporal usefulness.

In sentient dive the eagle
joins the epic survival act,
in repeat, timelessly again.

The theoretical nihilism, defined
by special interests of diverse
groups and movements,

persistently attempt to engineer
linguistic transformations to
disguise the truth of existence's ways.

As the eagle intercepts the
rattlers' prey, its talons
close the jack's fated end.

The vacant views and absent logics
of the post-modernist's children
contrast with the witness of events.

The deep ecology, eco-feminist,
holistic health, new age mysticism,
and global ecological consciousness

movements, all of fairly noble intent,
but baseless biological understanding,
reject naturalist awareness.

How they contrast in stark opposition,
to the simple act of nature's
creatures in wildness act exposed.

As the rattlers speed to
landscapes of new opportunities,
the eagle soars to offspring's nest.

The fecund rabbits' breeding
will insure the balance maintains,
not human intervention nor intent.

Survival of the fittest is nature's choice,
and not man's to make, we are of
nature and not apart or above.

The theorists who reject empiricism
and evidence, are blind to the mandate
of nature's knowing way; and

would destroy the foundation of
biologically inspired adaptation and
response in evolution's course.

As nightfall's curtain slowly
fades the majesty of colored
sands and native flowers,

the stillness closes upon
a sunless pebbled floor,
the immensity of eons restored.

Conservation is not intervention, our
forecast of consequences poor, and
those convinced otherwise-- dangerous.

For the nihilistic, narcistic,
paganistic, socially constructed and
interpretative mode will not endure.

Just as the desert moon, provides
the cycle of relent, it spawns the
truth of observation's sage.

Truth slanted or perverted to
accommodate the social myths
of technology's alienated age

and romantic zeal, will not long
sustain the scrutiny of the common
core, for they are the realists, the

fulcrum of the conscious plentitude,
upon whom nature's memory
leans and lends its vital store.

II.

And as creation's glory
spends the night, with luminous
stars and heavens cast in light,

one would be remiss to
contradiction's greatest fail to engage;
its spiritualist's lie and grave mistake.

The mistaken choice of theocrats
who seek to merge the worlds of
faith and reason in common blur.

For just as cactus close their blooms
to night, for lesser reason minds
are closed against the light.

The failed creed as biblical truth
be told is moved to science's stage,
were logic's searing does obtain.

And in this harsh terrain, the logic
dies, the staircase to heaven's door,
crumpled by the weight of science's eye.

Some argue every advance is science
by mystics told, as Kuhn's misreading
now as eastern mysticisms unfold.

Some say all medicine is as herbal gifts,
of godly summons to the earth's
resplendent past and ecological thrift.

But the dysfunctional logic is precisely
that, a mirror of post-modern reflect,
a Nostradamus prescience in disguise.

The true believers go one better still
in their desperate plight, as biblical
assertions lay shattered by the facts.

They substitute some version of
the word "god", for every new prime
mover or causal agent which is found.

But in the still and clear of wondrous
nights, the desert tells true the
beautiful story of life's real journey.

The lucid Martin Gardner responds
giftedly, by revealing all the errors
of categorical thinking in his test.

Of four anthropic principles does
he list, which nicely sum as "revelations"
consistent with the theocrat's favored gist.

The four can be seen as interpretative
claim, that they each gain strength of
form and as next is framed:

The Weak Anthropic Principle, or WAP,
tells us through god's agency,
the "universe allows us to exist".

The Strong Anthropic Principle, or SAP,
posits that "the existence of life
explains the laws of the universe".

The Participatory Anthropic Principle, or PAP,
postulates that "conscious observers are
necessary to bring the universe into existence".

The Final Anthropic Principle, or FAP,
concludes that "if life or consciousness ends,
the universe will immediately cease to exist".

To these startling flights of post-
modernist thinking, a stew in theocratic
garb and social political correctness,

the mischievous Martin adds a fifth
anthropic principle, whose acronym alone
brings glee and supreme joy to the thoughtful.

The Completely Ridiculous Anthropic Principal,
or CRAP, which is a self-evident reply
to anyone who buys into any of the first four.

III.

So it is upon this moonlight repose of
partitioned thought, at journey's end
of undivided mind, one can rest.

Believing that the best of knowledge
is in our future attainable, separable
from the viper's deadly nest.

For though the rattlers' venom is acute,
the birth of mind is nature's greatest gift,
and we will overcome the great untruth,

as eagles soaring mightily above the mist,
awaiting moments sacred in themselves,
of nature's doing and of nothing else.

DARK RETREATS

In crevices of the hillside,
icy folds protect,
the contents of our past.

The mind dispelled in fragments,
a songline of creation,
of consciousness in layers.

The reptile's cunning instinct,
its lack of gradient choice,
uninhibited by restraint.

No maternal string,
a numbers game of chance,
a deadly killer eye.

A radiant moon reveals,
the stillness of intent,
unbridled by remorse.

Survival of a module,
speciation cast aside,
reinforces the selfish gene.

In the heavens of the mind,
emotion clouds the trail
of descent and regress.

As the truth gets nearer,
the fears intrude again,
to pronounce nature blind.

ELEMENTS

Numbers, atoms, molecules,
and the notes of music heard,

colors of the spectrum hum,
the strings of nature's amplitude.

A forest dark, primeval threads,
hidden by the shadow's claim,

the theme of life, as dust renewed,
buried in discordant pain.

A computation, as pure element,
the basis of all fate,

the process of the universe,
immune to joy, and blind to state.

And yet the beauty springs to life,
amid the blindness and the strife,

for in the art and musical strains,
consciousness--- the meaning---

obtains and sings triumphant!

FRAGMENTS

The monk transcendent,
blue stones livid,
the fractal nested
in the mind's reflection.

The noise is pierced
by luminous moments,
fragments separated, the
immensity of nothingness.

Understanding scale, hidden
detail, shaded masks,
only faintly lift the
clouded misty veil.

How does the sea
of mind, find an
essence of something,
a fundamental construct,

tangible meanings in
submerged dark waters
of unknowing, disguised
as waves of experience?

INFERTILITY

The dark matter of the mind,
torments deep the inner self.

The need, for purpose and
supreme being,

the myths and shrines,
of the transcendent death,

evolution's salve, now
maturity's arrest and regress.

The universe now reveals,
the vast unseen in luminosity,

the immensity of that, which
comprises most of what is.

The soil's spent, a barren world,
evolution's brutish sport,

galaxies ever-distant, propelled
beyond the abyss.

The primate's fears of
nature's gory night,

innate as language itself,
the module of belief.

But through the veil,
the spectre looms,

and heaven's furrows
seem as doomed,

for can it be, that
yet we shall clearly see,

the grass as stellar gas,
carbon bi-peds emerging,

and no tree growing in
our mythical heaven?

SECRET GARDEN

In the wet wiring, patterns emerge,
as cascades of intentional strings.

Mappings in fold, image and symbol
retold, of tokens in processing rings.

Fuzzy boundaries, multiple sets,
the properties of ambiguities singing.

How does the brain, extract the
features across dissimilar regions?

Fractals and fragments, alive in the
soup, electrons and chemicals mixing?

Eliminative constructs, the signaling
processes, the substrate of who we are?

What words may describe, to
anneal the divide of interpretive feedback?

The representations abstracted, the
referential pointers impacted,

the dynamics obscured by the stew.

Interactions still masked, the virtual task,
immune to reductionist view.

The static impart, the state of the art,
unable to simulate the embrace.

A society needed, for referential affirm,
the self in relation to others.

The physics observed, changed by act
of the act, a framework of worthy recover.

The cosmos is said, contains dimensions
in layers, unavailable to practical capture,

intrinsic qualia, representational experience,
the self-referential enrapture.

The recursive shapes in parallel states,
the asynchronous-synchronous process,

all point to universe, much richer than
cosmic, with implications for research.

Exploring the quantum, contextual
logics, of collaboration's possible setting,

consciousness complex, disruptive
geometries, mathematical topos vetting.

Current equations, algorithmic evasions,
too brittle and much too mundane,

analogies too vapid, hardware to software,
the computational model's dull render.

Tool as artifact, no hierarchical depth,
a simplistic metaphorical swaddle,

innovation vamped, alert to the heat,
the hammer in useless re-dredging.

For the secret is mute, from the
garden remand, the translucent

mind unseen in the hedging,
the strings are alert to complexity's

song, as the universe laughs---
at cognitive science's undressing.

NAOMI'S OLIVE GROVE

The moon rises over the silk road,
the self-interrupting visionary stoic,
the ocean of sand silently watching
and waiting as ghosts worship in dance.

The black-cloaked figure casts no scent,
discernible shadows absent in colored
dust, death at sunset masking love's
purity, the oasis waters as clear and still.

The mystical imaginings traverse sorrowfully,
the ghazals of antiquity in serenity pose,
as the ordinary is made equal to the magical,
and voices from minarets fill the void.

The waterwheel's creak, evaporates the
pretensions of sacred infinities and
the messianic wish, the blue liquid
indulgences of sin-eaters in dining.

Is it the flesh of immortals and the
disgust of their vengeance hidden,
as demons of reason's betrayal?
Or do dervishes whirl in resignation?

As the mystical dance transcends the
extent, do the atoms unfurl in apostolic
delight; or is the ecstasy born of
stark revelations as magical lanterns,

illuminating patterns invisible to our
senses in vertiginous repeal?
Do the squalls of the electrons, dizzying
spin, hide horizons immune to apostasy?

The curvature of the mind is no
less the curvature of space-time,
as spiral galaxies equilibrate the
cosmic picture of our understanding.

Do the tails of the monster invariably
get cannibalized, by gigantic
black holes of our imagination, to
provide the material of our reincarnation?

Or does the plunge into the abyss, the
black hole of ignorance, swallow
our consciousness, as gravity feasts on the
material constituency of our existence?

Perhaps, knowledge on the abyss,
face-to-face with itself, is the meaning
of itself, giving itself its own unique
signature of destruction's meaning to existence?

Pure knowledge on the horizon of
its own death, must inevitably
seek its own death, for renewal to
have meaning and meaning to have essence.

How can the circle be unbroken, if
the circle has no bound or center?
Is there a core without a centrosome,
or is the center everywhere simultaneously?

Perhaps the mystical search is mistaken,
the door of the sanctuary is its exit, the
entrance residing in the present, and the
glorious extravagance of truly being conscious?

STARGAZING

The path we seek,
in our dreams,

radiant energy unfolding,
a microwave scent.

The absurdity of darkness,
matter and image,

unseen dimensions,
gas and particles,

hidden in backgrounds,
of ebony cold.

What will it mean,
the discovery unveiled,

in fragmented hues,
we can't comprehend?

A cold mountain home,
a sliver of moonbeam,

a spare little hut,
a knowing of singleness?

A particle point,
a measure of self,

the cosmos of strings,
a chorus unheard?

In some higher state,
the dark is unrobed,

the spotlight reveals,
the categories trace.

Into musical laws,
a vibrating art

of colors reveals
the spectrum of chance,
arrayed in dimensions
of immensity's foam.

For those who embrace
the realms of reflect,

beyond static bounds,
and linear fields,

in dynamic colors
and palettes of feeling,

that live in shadows
of senses yet evolved.

A REMARKABLE FABRIC

Our connection to nature,
a deep purple glow,

image without words,
the feel of the river.

Each creature alone,
a definable path,

conscious in layers,
the dust of stars.

We still do not know,
how thought occurs,

deep in a system,
the wetware of mind.

Is the expression of
something, ever vacant

of an image, the
sense and the feeling,

the perception or
known word?

As simple as it seems,
we are without knowing,

two different dimensions,
of consciousness and

memory, the fire and
the rain, the beat

of the drum, and the
wilderness of fragments.

The fabric is woven,
in splendid arrangement,

unique to the creature,
the nature of role.

We make the circle,
of corn and tobacco,

and offering to spirits
a protection to home.

The eagle soars, for
the majesty of being,

to search and to honor
the gift of flight.

How will the science,
unravel the mystery,

so tightly bound
to representational things?

Will ever the molecules,
lay open their secrets,

the twine of knitting,
devoid of their spin?

DESERT FLOWERS

Awareness of the blossoms, the coyote's
deep howl, the colors in the background,
engulfed in mountain squalls.

How do we take it in, the fragments of
our space, the billion firing neurons,
the self at center place?

The separate little structures, the
filaments of our brain, in unified
smooth concert---the binding.

We see the purple hillside, the layered
hues of spring, the eagle soaring skyward,
the ephemeral shimmering wing.

We share it with each other, the thought
and words congeal, reality corresponding
to the visual field----the grounding.

The debate abjures unending, amidst
elusive streams, focus or the
sentient response, illusive as a dream.

Our thoughts of our own origin,
controlling center stage, or illusions
of our fancy, behaviors and the rage.

The Cartesian theater, the deterministic
claim, or a subtle older context,
free will, its other name---agency.

WITHOUT JUDGMENT

On an iron mountain,
lie the ashes of battle,
and the echoes of defeat.

No light on heroic deeds,
warms the air, or
illuminates the feathers.

A solemn breath, ushers in
each reigning moment
of observed reflect,

each creature of the
present, feels the anguish
of the sacred place.

The moment's scars,
still hide within
the tortured crevices

of memories divide,
between dimensions of
the time and layers.

Layers of mind, in
vast dimensions,
hidden from observe,

open only,
to emotive refrains,
of unconscious summons.

No magistrate, but
nature's call,
bids selection's choice,

all categories, abstracts of
evolution, the progress
of individual mind.

Consciousness, an embodiment,
of the physical process
in experience's whole,

experience and meaning,
development and circuitry,
growing as learning,

interpreting and rendering
unique design, the feedback trace,
the dynamic tree.

A shaman's circle, gives
to meaning, the warm
ecstatic embrace,

the ritual context,
representative hue,
but understanding is opaque.

Categories open to refute,
and re-shaping, as fiery circles
of myths and chants,

appeal to senses, and to
the heart, but not
to force of logic's rant.

Epistemology, grounded in
biology, especially neuroscience
applies the scope,

to salient features, parts and
fragments, fractal patterns in
mosaic splendor.

But from all this,
no song emerges,
of described notes;

for notes alone, do not
reveal the symphonies'
melodies, or emotional grace.

The hearing separates the
thought from thinking,
the sound from itself,

the primal meaning,
the mind's own filter
for understanding's embrace.

It is in the wholeness,
of ourselves, that we
create our unique thoughts.

No functionally separate,
unconnected parts, escape
the systems' wiring.

A network of networks,
our invent, perhaps a
token to our regime?

Near Khe Sanh plateau,
upon a ridge, the stillness
meets leaden skies.

The Lang Vei camp,
the iron mountain,
in its weeping still.

Thousands died, on
both sides, for the
so-deemed key terrain,

but now, their youth
and souls, reside in caged
molecular stains.

Those that abound,
in memories' clouds,
dimension our dreams,

etched by the trauma,
of the battles, and reinforced
by all the tears.

The circuitry of consciousness,
the tapestry of fears,
the fabric of the mind's divide,

the cumulus of the years,
all remembrances of conflicts
waste, misguided gloried tales,

through the veil seared by fire,
bodies thrown upon the pyre,
and the weight of history's scale.

The iron mountain sits alone,
to all but experienced soul,
the molecules alone regret,

the tragic spiritual toll,
the mind the only resting place,
of the unknown dead,

whose spirits roam these
solemn hills, absent of breaths
so freely given and taken.

THE PLATEAU

On a windy plain,
immune to the modern sound,
an idea spreads.

Is it a voice,
or just invisible fractal,
a wisp of smoke?

The mountains obscure,
the folded horizons of
the conscious mind.

The computation's music,
is lost in the sentient noise
of everyday living.

Perhaps, it must be, or
the vast categories of things
would overwhelm the senses,

and the essence of all
would be forever hidden,
as is the mystery?

If the sacred is obvious,
does the quest of knowing
diminish its essence?

To smell, feel and hear
nature's wise breath,
is to know of eternity,

if not here, then all
the other places where
life must surely exist,

and will exist, if not now,
but as before and then, as is
the destiny of the cosmos.

THE VANISHING SELF

Soon enough will come
the day of our death,

the consciousness of the meadow,
lost to eternity.

A hunter of invisible prey,
discovery and meaning,

moved to the other side
of the mirror.

When the monastery bell tolls,
the separateness

of self will no longer
obtain,

a flash of being untangled
no more.

Now just part of the "it",
the great mystery,

folded once again, in the
particles and waves,

the robed cosmos of
of the infinite.

In the immensity of truths,
a mere handful--

as the wind blows away
our footprints,

and only the sands of time
truly endure.

WAITING AND LISTENING

Blankly staring, as
the Lama chants, intoning
soft vibrations,

timeless ritual,
sounds of ancient edification,
real or imagined.

Does inspiration float, as
some metamorphic plasma,
idea particles--

barely formed factoids,
settling as random pinpoints
of ashen specks,

meditative flickers, a residue
of humanity's consciousness,
shards of memes?

How is the concept
formed, and transmitted, from
pyramids and mounds,

observatories and the mathematics,
to glyphs, signs, higher languages;
synchronously emergent,

presumably without
direct contact and transcription,
disconnected in space?

The archaeologist, evolutionist,
and geneticist, all have
convincing models,

particulars and scenarios,
to explain the process of invention
and development,

but they posit little,
to explain the synchronicity of
form and timeline?

In a formerly unconnected
world, absent and isolated
in its vastness,

deemed uncontaminated
and unreachable by
oceanic travel,

punctuated cultural and
developmental features of
major advances

occur, almost simultaneously,
in disparate civilizations-- so say
these expert researchers.

The factoids are convincing,
but the explanations are wanting,
or virtually non-existent.

So, dear reader,
I continue to ask, as
the chant master's hymns

seek to transport me
through the fabric of my
own unreality,----how

does the non-local entanglement
of evolved ideas voyage across
the dimensionality

of space-time and place,
to create the birth of imitation's
next child?

Is it mere serendipity---or
a natural progression of archetypes,
a predestined emergence?

Plato and Bohm smile, as
Newton and Einstein frown,
strings dancing merrily aloof.

IV. SOLITUDES AND AMPLITUDES

CROSSROADS

The red dust cakes the brittlebush,
a sign of the passing wind,
from the east---the devil wind
the Mexicans called it.

From this lookout two trails seen,
a decision of the heart,
not the mind, the vacant mind,
captive to the force of fate.

How cheaply life was valued then,
when in our youth adventure
and pride weighed so heavily,
passion crushing reason's voice.

We claimed there was no choice,
no choice that honor or integrity
would allow, or could allow,
us so committed to the cause.

It's only now, in dreams of disbelief,
that absent muses of a voice's echo,
and in the face of death's remorse do
we reflect and stare into the void.

Did we suspect, but just not care?
Can we ever know the landscape's
map of choices, flowing wildly in
the stream of our own self's discontent?

Or are we forever condemned to think
we decide in some rational space,
weighing facts and parsing options,
a conscious method of choice and act?

If only that were true, there is little
doubt that judgment's way would prevail,
and acts then followed would be undone,
the footprints at the crossroads still.

For there is path of no choice, often
overlooked in passion's rush and
desperation's fury, where peace
and wisdom can and does prevail.

A FRIEND'S DEATH

The call came,
late one night,

the battle over,
the last breath taken.

The cancer spread,
from prostate to

lymph nodes, to bone
and vital organs.

Two years of pain
and courage,

valiant striving to
the inevitable end.

All the cocktails
of modern medicine,

radiation and chemical,
couldn't arrest the onslaught.

"It's a shame he died",
said one.

"No it's a blessing",
said another.

Chief Blue Coyote
would have wondered,

"Did he have time
to go to the mountain,

and talk to his spirit,
before he slept" ?

Sometimes I wonder,
whom amongst us

are the most wise,
the ghosts of yesterday's

meaning, the carriers
of the songline;

or the prophets of
today's conventions,

the men without souls
or painted faces.

STORMY WEATHER

The grey bitter wind
reminds the elderly man
of his dissatisfaction in knowing.

In knowing of myths revealed,
as chains of divergent paths
amidst the rubble of certainty's rainbow.

In knowing of fate's cunning
as smiles hidden in relief of
golden harvests of contingency's choice.

In knowing that one's love
is conditional, as disrobed by denials
of inattention and vacant understanding.

The rains in punctuated torrents
drench the feelings of content
and drown happiness in despair,

disproving the adage of
discovering virtue, in the
nakedness of life's imperfection.

AMBITION

The reticent man smiles obliquely,
the dissipation of joyfulness
traveling the lines of his countenance.

Solemnity born of suspicion, tragedy
of character and impoverishment
of noble cause, and not knowing of oneself.

He has achieved high office and seeks
even higher--- the penultimate goal
of political dreams and intentioned schemes.

Were his motives as pure as the naive believe,
or has the erasure of time and the lies
of the intelligentsia masked the disgrace?

How many of his brethren were willfully pained,
by his slander and generalizations,
in unremitting pursuit of his personal cause?

Were his beliefs ever genuine, his facts ever
compelling, his sources of accusation ever
found wanting or purposefully untrue?

The histories there, but seldom revisited
of opportunism's trail and the collaborations
made within a journey of betrayal.

Of all that is sacred in honor's great cause,
the virtue of freedom and defense of
its stepchildren in democracies march,

the totalitarians and apologists still slither
in the shadows of noble refrains of
progressive anthems and revolutionary dress.

But the walls keep on falling of failed
experiments, the attempt to coerce
what the tanks of October could not wrest away.

Only the elitists in garb of the people,
still cling to politics of economic scarcity,
of opportunities inequality through bloody redress.

Some say he has changed, it was only his youth,
he more carefully chooses his causes and friends,
but the record speaks loudest in military affairs,

where again for extremism he has made no amends.
In almost all issues where support was most needed he
voted with those whose conscience is naught.

His new-found compassion for all in our service
ring hypocritical as commitment, as empty as
the spare parts and stores that were voted against.

Do we care for integrity, character and record?
Or are we so used to celebrity and deceit such that
sincerity is mistrusted and courage so feared?

His artifacts of performance, his new
smile much intact, give hope to the
faithful whose immorality is immune to attack.

The free ride they give to the molester
of interns, the place in their hearts
for the queen of hilarious pause,

gives those who take serious the threats
to our freedom, our institutions of pride,
and the international terrorists' cause;

and no reason for believing our children
are safe from the ravages of ideology
and the barbarity of the elitist's estate.

He sent an appeal to the "Band of Brothers",
those Vietnam-era veterans he so
unashamedly courted and summarily abused.

The liars and addicts will heed the call,
but it is hoped that the accusations of
the dead, and those who nobly served

will drown out the chorus of cancer
and respond to the lie; and who as the real
heroes of our country's political shame

will not be silent in history's refrain,
but will denounce with one voice this
defamer--- never retiring the battle!

THE REAL WAR

It screams at me,
each night, alone and
lost in the glare,

not where our children
are falling, but
close, in the memeplex,

where the idea is born,
supported by their poets,

in a language we don't
understand, and of a religion

many misrepresent.

This medieval impulse is
reborn, purity of raiment,

substituting for criticality
of thought, for knowledge
and expertise,

belief suspended in time,
the love of irrationality,

death as purification,
to atone for failure.

The failure of a civilization,
to renew itself in spirit,
to bring merit to its place,

recapture its identity, and
restore learning to its faith.

It is at the site of the
great prophet, that this war
will be won,

not by guns or aliens, but
only through the wisdom,

the courage and the learning,
of the people's trusted sons.

DO YOU KNOW THIS MAN?

Have you seen the face of death?
I have and he isn't really that scary.

But I have seen the face of morbidity
And though they both share some eerily
Similar features, I find him truly worrisome.

Morbidity is extraordinarily tall, with grey ashen
Skin like latex, beneath his hooded eyes.

The imagined scythe he translucently wields is
Unimpressive, more like rust coated iron, than the steel blue
Icy scimitar of rapier sharpness you would expect.

He seems cold like his eyes, which are seemingly always filled with
Disappointment and regret, even when he is smiling.

And he does occasionally smile, but even then it appears
Forced and unnatural, he appears wounded by the effort.

His chin is long, and one eye noticeably droops toward it,
Lower than the other, as if it must always be wary of the
Melancholy in all things, least temporary joy turn to optimism.

There is no spring to his gait, long and trodden,
His shoulders droop in dejected resignation.

He seems to want you to respect him, not fear him
Or like him, but he is too ill at ease and unsure
Of his essence for you to do either.

He has done his duty both past and present with
Some honor it is told, but there are lingering doubts.

Was he sincere in the aftermath of service, or an
Opportunist seeking to profit from the chaos
And advantage by the winds of change?

Are his beliefs, his values and positions, things grounded
In principle, or merely wind ripples on the sail's fabric?

His grasp of the texture of people's spare lives, are they
Real, or a flag that he waves to be loved?

Is his need to be shown the affection he craves,
A premise of leadership, or a narcissistic cross?

Will how he got to be who he is, or what he pretends to be,
Portend a prelude toward merit, or a recipe for tragedy?

How will he fare when he faces alone, those issues
Of life, and of right and of wrong; decisions often
Made in the glare of unpopular choice?

Will he discard the worn baggage of populist script
And recognize the true fundamentals of this nation's
Strengths, the source of its equality in opportunity?

Will he support the freedoms that drive its engines
Of commerce and make it the beacon of light for
The world's immigrating rivers of aspirants?

Will he rein-in the power of both the behemoths
And the law makers who exact the hidden burden
That threatens the lifeblood of our collective ethic?

Or will he evacuate the bowels of leadership
And the Nation's welfare to be embraced by
Extremists of his own clan, still living in darkness?

Will he have the courage to face down
Those who would dictate, indoctrinate and "plan",

Who claim monopoly on truth, correctness, and
Care, but dream to control unfazed by the failed
Experiments, miseries and the myths of the past?

It certainly is time for a principled man---neither
Dogmatist nor faith-healer. A man who
Knows himself and the true nature of liberty's way.

Is he that man? Will he reveal himself?
We do not know---------and only time will tell.

A WONDERFUL PERSON

Sometimes in the smile of innocence,
you sense a deeper presence,
a faculty for seeing colors
invisible to the common sight.

But too often the mirror has no reflection,
the clear lines no routes and signposts,
and the map is all surface mask,
without a depth of meaning or referral.

How does one come to this place?
a being of childish grace, uncritical
mind afloat on shimmering light,
in a wave-less pond of shallow imitation?

Is the path of knowing, the undoing?
Does the music in the mist obscure
the connections and choices there,
or are the chords of dissonance innate?

THE LAST PERFORMANCE

The puppet master reels,
from the devastating loss,
his finest and final act,
drawn to permanent close.

The filament has torn,
the severed distance grows,
freedom's bell intoned,
rebuke is now disclosed.

It was a sustained run,
a manic tour de force,
of manipulative excess,
behaviors wily gamed.

It succeeded while in youth,
before identities were cast,
but as wisdom re-affirmed,
the pathology was defamed.

For loyalty is not bequeathed,
in entitled inheritance,
guilt in treacherous sleeve,
an impermanent countenance.

In the final scene,
a naked cruel petard,
disparaging memory's light,
of a loved one in regard.

Unsympathetic sleights, and
unmitigated scorn,
excuses without love,
slander with the facts.

It could not hold in bond, the
players and the script,
the brazen lie was false,
as were the ugly quips.

The lesson was now learned,
liberty must be obtained,
freedom must be earned,
the primal need sustained.

IMPERMANENCE AND SOLITUDE

A gentleman has died,
we grieve at our collective loss.

A life of work and care,
for loved ones and the task,

unaffected by the tribute,
the stature or the mask.

It was enough to sense
the joy, of dearly endured friends,

of family and recourse to all,
the every-day simple things.

Coursing through a world,
of vast uneven trends,

piloting a ship, of dutiful
mundane events,

it is hard to say the words
of adequate import.

No strident moral cause,
no singular great rejoice,

an even thoughtful keel,
a fair reflective voice.

But the curmudgeon will be
missed, his uniquely droll replies,

to almost any shout,
pronouncement— claim or lie.

"Too hard, too simple, it makes
my head hurt---

too suspicious, too fair---
obvious, trite, or inert."

An oft heard reply, a
categorical claim,

of feigned indifference, to
pomposity and to sage.

But after the jolt,
the appeal to sense,

the dissection would come,
as worthy recompense.

A thoughtful man, not
given to reveal,

the spin zone was lethal,
the narcissist's heal.

Occam's own razor,
dull in repair,

to Thomas's tongue,
and his rueful deep glare.

He is gone to the shadows,
the myths of the mind,

no need for Valhalla
or imaginary shrine.

And though mystery of death
may elude us all,

it is safe to reveal, that
he answered the call,

of giving meaning to life,
and love to those held close,

he was a man for his season,
so to him we do toast.

MISTAKEN IDENTITY

A vacant man, with empty eyes,
an affected stare, of arrogant reprise.

How was he then, when she was young?

A ruthless man, of self-import,
feigning tears, mining dark fears.

How was he then, when she was young?

In later years, the truth is known,
what masked it all, for so long?

Who was he then, when she was young?

It's over now, the wisdom's gained,
all the years, spent in vain,
the price was high, the emotive pain.

Who was he then, when she was young?

He sits alone, in emptied room,
his new bride waits, in saddened gloom,
the cycle sees, another day,
how long before, she will say---

Who is he now, this man I married?

A 21ST CENTURY SYMPHONY

First Movement

The Mozart adagio, in repose,
the Stravinsky piece, introducing
a fledgling modernity.

The 20th Century's tumult revealed,
prior to institutional atrocity,
the ugly new stain.

What viral pattern of
memetic rampage, propagates
the breadth of search?

The poets incline to remorse,
the ugly prejudice toward science
and embrace of pseudo-science,

---or the de-constructionist's folly,
the relativist's shallow illogic,
robed as gnosis?

Outside on the street,
the protesters gather, neuro-scientific
research, their enemy of the day.

Utopian zeal, sociological
blather, economic illiteracy,
must all play their part.

But what do historians say,
and what do historians know,
beyond the truly banal?

Another century dawns, the
music discordant, the therapist's
folk-tales still in misuse.

The academic irrelevancies,
concerned with the tangential,
scholarship mutant and impotent,
amidst socio-therapeutic chum.

The world is yet divided, by
the wealth of the mind,
and the uncritical razor,
of ideological strife.

Some say the internet, will
close the vast chasm, but how
do you surf through the flotsam
of uncritical noise?

Choose any University, browse
through the courses, search for
a curriculum, that may offer
some lucidity. What do you find?

Communications, gender studies,
political science {is it really science},
mythology and metaphysical studies,
yuk! --- New Age epistemology?

Cringe at the syllabus, few
hard sciences, no literature of meaning,
logic or critical thinking, scant
mathematics or economics,
----and let's all avoid biology!

My God, what of poetry?
Who needs poetry?

Second Movement

You see my friends, it is neither
racist nor insensitive,
to angrily proclaim,
that even amongst the most
homogenous cultures,

some tribes and micro-cultures,
are warped bastions of belief,
injurious to democracy, rancid
in behavioral implication.

To judge comparatively, with
critical hindsight, is required.
To be value focused, without
western-centric prejudice is possible.

Some "micro-cultures", like native
gangs and criminal enterprises, are broken:
socially pathological, and value-deprived,
and that should be indisputable.

Historically, some indigenous tribes,
of both the Americas, were labeled,
with strong evidence, to be untrustworthy
and venal by their indigenous neighbors.

That was not a western-centric opinion, or
insensitive---it was mere reflect of local facts,
a common sense view about what types
of behaviors, at any stage of development
are normative and acceptable.

No anthropologically accurate, nor
hemisphere-neutral viewpoint exists free of
values, internally or externally.
Multi-culturalism is a cop-out, like Rogerian
therapy, we all use a standard or reference,

whether it is passive, neutral-seeking,
unbiased, or non-directive, since all data and
evidence is weighted against some criterion,
consciously or unconsciously---
by anthropologists, sociologists, therapists,
or mere observers of the phenomena.

Was there ever a more pre-disposed or
biased rendering of specious "data" than
that of Margaret Mead's Samoan paradise,
a construction of a reality which was

non-existent, and later proven purposefully
inspired by natives pandering to her biases?

Thus, one can always dispute, subjective
accounts and claim we bring our society's
or race's mental baggage to an encounter;
but more often recently, the bias has been
ideological, not cultural, a "going native"
syndrome predisposing a romantic view.

Regardless, this is a very slippery slope
for social scientists to tread, since
most of their field is circumstantial at best,
and most of the grievously trumped up and
distorted "data" has come from their work.

For them to criticize "factoids" and data
of other less predisposed observers is
disingenuous, at best ------and to brand
observations as "critical" or "insensitive"
merely because they call into question

locally normative beliefs, of isolated
tribes and micro-cultures, is vapid.
I am sorry, mutilating a woman's sexual
"componentry" to satisfy religious,
cultural, or tribal belief is "barbaric"!

Other charges, like racism or specious
genetic/eugenic slanders are equally
without foundation, and show the extremes
to which many of these intellectual
pretenders will go to further their agenda.

For it is uncontested that those born into
disconnected cultures, share the same genetics
as all other cultures, but some researchers have
been criticized for merely pointing out that from
the time of their birth, their behaviors and beliefs

have been delimited by their environment,
which that sadly means, that in extremely
disconnected cultures, these beliefs and modes

of conduct, are even more largely intransigent
and reflective of a limited intra-cultural self.

Whatever minor access, or experiences,
they may have to outside influences, by way
of travel and interaction with dissimilar
micro-cultures, in the externally larger world,
there is still a cultural lack of diversity in
their stimulation and in their "becoming".

Third Movement

This phenomena exists everywhere in
every culture, except that in the era of mass
communication, it is harder to find on the
surface of socialization, especially in the
developed and emerging world of modern
communities.

And though the world views of the individual
can be altered, in the most value-disconnected
voids of the isolated group's larger complex,
insertion of evolved ideas seems to have little
effect on group dynamics, as is daily witnessed
and observable of most micro-cultures.

Thus, though individuals may be well
intentioned and integrated, the group
dynamic is the fundamental force, and
normative bound, particularly in dysfunctional
isolated cultures.

So, largely disconnected, means precisely
that---not often being a part or in touch with
the people and or ideas of other cultures
and diverse groups, lacking in feedback-rich
personal interactions with those groups.

A condition that exists, not because
of capitalism, imperialism, colonialism,
the lack of educational opportunities, or
any other litany of victim-directed causes.

For the easy- label conventional wisdoms,
do not hold up to the tests of experience
or statistical dynamics. Look carefully
at the history of racism in our culture, and
the decades of transformational failure.

Racism, while being historically valid as
a causal agent for micro-culture dysfunctionality,
today is being viewed differently, especially
by a newer Black, well-educated community;
and fewer and fewer Afro-American thinkers

believe that it can be viewed as the major
causal agent---especially as it applies to the
plight of younger Black men in the inner city,
which is why it is an exemplar of a cultural
problem that is more complex.

In all value-deprived cultures, the effects
are prolonged, largely because people
who live in value-deprived cultures,
absent of economic and personal freedom,
disconnected from modernity, where education

is de-valued, are also often in communities
deficient in the rule of law, and an informed
community of interest. This makes them
more susceptible to a layer of beliefs and
behaviors that are negatively and recursively
reinforcing.

Whether describing a gang-dominated
slum community, a feudal village in a warload
controlled Middle-Eastern country, or a lawless
favela in Latin America, the poverty is of values first,
and then economics and opportunities secondly.

Mexico, as an example, is full of villages
that have endemic poverty, but strong values, and
few of the other woes of disconnected communities.
Thus, they have an industrious culture of emergent
modernity without most of the negative attributes.

In fact, in many of these value-deprived communities,
it is not poverty but the wealth of illegal and criminal
opportunities with impressive rewards, that lure the
bright young leaders, seducing them from traditional
paths of advancement and opportunities.

So, history always plays a role, but many
generations later, it is intellectually
dishonest to continue beating poverty and
racism as the prime drum of causality.
Values do matter, and value-free multicultural
nonsense is a barrier to a culture's emergence.

The African-American community, again is
an exemplar within America, of the battle lines
in these cultural wars, and is the mainstream
in its opposition to the media and its embrace
and exploitation of young Black men being
driven by the values and images of the hip-
hop micro-culture.

The African-American community has
experienced impressive economic gains and
employment mobility, with unprecedented
numbers of men and women now in the upper
middle and middle classes and living in
diverse integrated communities.

It is they, those upwardly mobile highly
educated Black Americans who are fighting
a valiant war about values, beliefs,
stereotypes, gender belittlement, racial profiling,
self-reinforcing negative behaviors, and images
in this battle with Hollywood and Black
entertainment moguls.

To them, part of the problem in the leave-behind
community, appears to be that this old
stereotypical and negative behavior is being
reinforced, and rewarded economically, while
the new model for advancement and progress,
namely education, is being ridiculed. This reverses
the progress of affirmative action!

Within the next few years it will be courageous
Black leaders, educators, and entrepreneurs
who will change the old culture and
transform it to the new---and they and
only they, can successfully fight that battle.

Similar battles are raging even within
non-democratic communities, as the
next decade will see the broader Asian world
evolve to become an economic, and yes,
more slowly, democratic European-like
community.

Communism is evolving to Mandarin-like
authoritarianism, but that won't last, as
economic freedom remakes the cultural
landscape and connectivity obtains.
Yet some of the similar problems with
integrating the connected and disconnected
worlds will persist, as rural disconnected
worlds and modern urban areas experience
a collision of norms and values.

Religious beliefs, ancient taboos and rituals,
tribal and pre-feudal systemic structures,
all contribute significantly to the Middle
East's endemic impoverishment, and
would continue unabated if our multi-
cultural value-free theology held sway.

The Middle East has an abundance of
resources, a rich history and an educated elite,
but is pre-capitalist and feudal in its practices,
its behaviors and psychological make-up; and
fundamentalist and extreme in its views,
which together are a prescription for barbarity.

True cultural poverty, exists today,
not as a primary result of access to
resources, but because of lack of access
to progressive shared values and behaviors,
a world of the under-educated, manipulated
youths held hostage to indoctrination.

The lack of connectivity to the modern world,
of progressive ideas, democratic and legal
rights as inalienable, and the leverage of
efficiency in agriculture, and technical
education that the entrepreneurial world enjoys,

is largely denied. As are the personal interactions
with diverse peoples, educational opportunities
and secular institutions of learning and commerce,
representing many different belief systems,
throughout the breadth and depth of society.

It is not governments that provide this interaction,
or advantage in knowledge and material, they
can only provide the environment within
which it can flourish or alternatively be
imprisoned or denied.

It is entreprenurism, protected and
encouraged by the government, which
begets the layered economic and social-
legal, self-generated infrastructure; which
as an emergent attribute of a complex

social dynamic, also creates the higher culture,
the means and tools of a creative society,
which can only be sustained by a populace
whose pervasive unconscious evolves
to embrace these values-- as inalienable.

It is, thus, mental impoverishment, that
fails to give rise to opportunistic estate,
a positive group dynamic, and the innate
expectation of fairness and civility, as a right.

In societies that are so evolved, diversity as
positive and invigorating, trust of law, and
the expectation of protection, are all
a part of a early consciousness.

Hence, throwing money or dubious
development projects at such cultures
or micro-cultures, is an impulse, unblemished
by success in our previous century---

especially when dealing with
those "nations" or "tribes", which are
merely religious "cults" or pretender
populist and activist movements.

These are "value-based" cultures, not
in the debased theological and restrictive
sense, but at a higher level of ethical and
moral consciousness, and commonwealth.

Fourth Movement

Ah, but what of these homegrown
"pretender" value-chains, the special
interest activists and their 'well-intentioned"
movements! Do they not aspire, the same?

Anti-globalization, anti-capitalism, anti-
big business, pro-vegetarian, PETA, pro-left
handed "Kayakers from Oregon Against
All Common-Sense Virtue and Values"?

These dear reader, are not the folks of
conscience, as during the civil rights marches,
nor the few that protested when the left ignored
Pol Pot slaughtering millions, or the Rwandans
bleeding to death in blood-soaked fields.

In historical fact, most, but not all, are merely
alienated remnants of the lunatic far left,
unmasked as unloved extremists, exposed
as mirrors of the same totalitarian pedigree,
which we have seen in the horrific past.

Inevitably opposed to the right of
the individual, the voice of liberty, anti-
democratic, and desperately anti-free
market, these folks espouse the "rights'
of various belief ideologies.

But they deny the world's underdeveloped and
disconnected-- the advantages of evolutionary

change, the rights of due process under law,
guaranteed personal freedoms, individual action,
as they deny these communities at large--- the
right to regulate their own internal affairs
and make their own choices.

They scream "haven't years of World Bank,
the Peace Corps, the International Monetary
Fund, and other intrusive endeavors, produced
essentially, more harm than good? It
must be capitalism! We dictatorial
intelligentsia know a better way!

Fifth Movement

Just to unmask this nonsense, really rankles
the elitist mentality, the sociological
theorists, Marxist economists, the
therapeutic narcissists, and "neo-humanists".

The "new activists", are really the same old
despisers of free trade, the popular culture, and
the inevitable chaos which democratic institutions,
and unbridled creativity creates.

Anti-globalization, anti-imperialism is the cry,
but the bitter truth is, that they, and many
of the other like-minded extremists, hiding
behind the shroud of mass hysteria share much.

Their movements, which so profess the love
of humanity—and protection of the pristine
wilderness, and each and everyone
of all the world's resplendent species—are
founded in common plight.

Not the fading of the indigenous world, or a
common sympathetic interest and resting place,
but the denial of evolving to a world in
which they themselves find no joy,
fulfillment, or identity.

Virtually all, special interest, ideological
mass movements, not founded on real
grievances or the pursuit of liberty, have
a common pathology amongst leaders, followers,
and rabid defenders.

Though they may be categorically different,
they are ontologically similar, to all the humorous
cults, as well as horrific mass movements of
history, especially those of our recent tragic past.

For we have seen them all before, history's morally
absolute, or nationally certain, gruesome utopian
or communal and social human re-engineering
experiments, all of which have
confused equality with fairness,

and led to some of the most heinous atrocities
of our time: to include the Gulag archipelago,
the killing fields of Cambodia, and even the
holocaust, aided by the pseudo-science of eugenics.

Their common leaders use hysteria, induced
through psychological babble, messianic rhetoric,
and spurious or blithely inane moral arguments,
to justify their acts of violence and ignorance.

Though new mass media, and its incredible
shallowness gives them seeming forums
of legitimacy today, which were denied
them in the past, their members are still of the
same psychological profile as earlier generations.

Largely composed of the idealistic, and
discontented, the "outsider" small minority,
insecure and often socially inept, if given
the chance, they always choose conformity within a
community of self-described non- conformists,
and oppression over liberty.

They are most often lead by the articulate, but
superficial intellectual-- outwardly charismatic,
vocally inspirational, and ultimately controlling,

who within that micro-culture appears moral,
and visionary.

But in truth, we know in the broader
context of socialization, these leaders are
the enfeebled and alone, the dissatisfied and
disassociated, at home only within
their claustrophobic world.

A world of self-distrust, adolescent conspiracy,
the unrequited hatred of all the other individuals
unlike them, who are adaptive to the wider
world of integrated emotions and normalcy.

Because in fact, they are typically amoral and
unethical, motivated by power, controlling,
self-absorbed, and only superficially engaged
as lovers of nature and humanity;

rewarded more by their group affiliation
than the merits of its cause---
cynical of individuals and discomforted
by nature as it really is---when its romantic
mask is removed.

Their followers are more often, just as inept,
emotionally disconnected--- but also the
simply very innocent, critically uneducated
dreamers--- lusting for commitment and purpose,
as easily seduced, as by any other cause.

Finale

So it is with great resignation, that the
symphony ends, with Stravinsky's discordance,
and the protester's confused dissonance
distressingly in common blend.

Two themes from the mists, of history's
wretched past, two hymns wildly different,
perhaps prophetically similar, haunt
the distributed regions of the mind.

Reminders of the cycle, infinite in its
regress, that reaches back through the
twilight to the edges of human time,
the sounds of the thumping apes.

The chimpanzee of words, still tumultuous
in evolution, no erudite of language,
overcoming the beast of evolution's
dawn, and the reptilian brain.

A snapshot is rendered, from trivial
pursuits, academics disrobed by the
mush that they offer for sustenance
of the mind in their pretender world.

The discord of logic, from Niagaras
of words, polemic nonsense, garbed
in an intellectual stew, unworthy of
taste and absent of substance.

What music will serve as the classical
brew, with the soul to survive,
that came from a century of death, in
vacant despair, apart from all meaning?

The future will tell, and may the harmonic
ring, with truth and with melody for
both the heart and brain, for it's a
melodious system we demand---
in the anthem's final refrain.